HOW TO RAISE AN OUTSTANDING PUP

WRITTEN & ILLUSTRATED BY
R.M. RIVAS

TO ALL MY LITTLE BEARS,
THANK YOU ONCE AGAIN
FOR ALL YOUR LOVE AND SUPPORT.

LITTLE BOOKS, BIG HEART
RMRIVAS.COM

HI, MY NAME IS BUTTONS AND THIS IS MY PAL BEAR!

LIFE CAN BE RUFF
WHEN YOU'RE RAISING A NEW PUP.

SO WE WROTE A NEW BOOK,
A HOW TO IF YOU WILL,

OF ALL THE FUN NEW RESPONSIBILITIES THAT COME WITH THE DEAL.

IT'S TOUGHER THAN IT LOOKS,
BUT WE KNOW YOU'LL DO GREAT.

SO BRING THAT EXCITEMENT WE SEE ON YOUR FACE,
IT'S TIME TO LEARN ABOUT WHAT IT TAKES.

I COULDN'T BELIEVE MY LUCK
THE DAY I FOUND OUT I GOT A NEW PUP!

I SMILED SO MUCH AT MY NEW LITTLE PAL,
IN MY HEAD I HAD ALREADY IMAGINED SO MANY TALES.

THIS PUP - RAISING ADVENTURE HAD JUST BEGUN,
I WAS READY
AND I WAS DETERMINED
TO RAISE A GOOD PUP.

TO START, BESIDES A GOOD NAME,
HE'D DEFINITELY NEED A WARM BATH,

SO I ROLLED UP MY SLEEVES
AND DID SOME QUICK MATH.
I NEEDED SOMETHING LITTLE WITH ENOUGH ROOM TO SPLASH.

I FILLED UP A SMALL TUB WITH BUBBLES AND SUDS,
THEN I PUT ON A RAINCOAT TO KEEP OUT ANY BUGS.

NEXT CAME HIS NAME AND THAT WASN'T BAD,
HE LOOKED LIKE A LITTLE BEAR AFTER HIS BATH.

IT WAS PERFECT, IT DESCRIBED HIM
AND THAT'S WHAT YOU WANT,
NOW ALL HE NEEDED WAS A COLLAR TO OFFICIALLY BE MY PUP.

WHEN YOUR PUPPY GETS HOME,

IT'S IMPORTANT TO MAKE HIM FEEL SPECIAL
WITH A SPOT OF HIS OWN.

IT DOESN'T NEED TO BE SUPER FANCY,

HIS OWN BUNDLED BLANKET WILL DO.

LET ME ALSO TELL YOU WHY YOU WANT TO STAY CLOSE BY.

EVERYTHING IS SO NEW,
IT MIGHT TAKE SOME TIME TO GET USE TO.
SO UNTIL HE SETTLES IN,
HE MIGHT KEEP CRYING
WHEN HE'S NOT RIGHT NEXT TO YOU.

NO NEED TO WORRY, THIS WON'T LAST LONG,
TRY READING HIM A BOOK OR LISTENING TO A SONG,

AND IN NO TIME AT ALL
YOU'LL BOTH BE SLEEPING ALL NIGHT LONG.

WHAT WILL THEY EAT?
I'M SO GLAD YOU ASKED.
NO CEREAL FOR THESE GROWING GUYS AND GALS.

NO

CIRCLE
OATS

MIL

NO PIZZA AND ABSOLUTELY NO JUNK!
WHAT YOUR PUP NEEDS,
TO GROW BIG AND STRONG
IS SOME GOOD OL' FASHION PUPPY CHUNKS.

PICK A GOOD KIBBLE THAT'S SOFT FOR LITTLE TEETH,
FILLED WITH VITAMINS, GOODIES AND LOTS OF TASTY MEATS.

THIS GIVES THEM WHAT THEY NEED
TO STRETCH OUT AND GAIN WEIGHT,
CAUSE PUPPIES LIKE BEAR, CAN GROW AT A REALLY FAST RATE.

DON'T FORGET FRESH WATER EACH AND EVERYDAY,
TO WASH DOWN THE KIBBLE BEFORE THEY PLAY.

THIS NEXT STEP IS THE TOUGHEST FOR SURE.
YOU'LL NEED LOTS OF TIME
AND PATIENCE GALORE.

PUPPIES LIKE BABIES, MAKE LOTS OF POO,
SO YOU'LL NEED TO PAY CLOSE ATTENTION
WHEN YOU WALK IN A ROOM.

TAKE YOUR PUP OUT TO POTTY
EVERY MORNING WHEN YOU WAKE,

AFTER EVERY MEAL THEY EAT,
AND RIGHT BEFORE THEY GO TO SLEEP.

ACCIDENTS ARE GONNA HAPPEN,
EVERYBODY MAKES MISTAKES.

JUST TRY NOT TO GET MAD
WHEN YOUR PUPPY DOESN'T PEE ON HIS PAD.

IT MIGHT TAKE A FEW DAYS,
IT MIGHT TAKE A FEW MONTHS,
BUT ONE DAY SOON YOU'LL HAVE YOURSELF
A POTTY TRAINED PUP!

THEY'LL NEED TO GO TO THE VET
TO GET THEIR CHECK UP,
SO DON'T FORGET!

JUST LIKE YOU AND I,
THEY'LL NEED A FEW SHOTS TO GET BY.

ONCE THAT'S ALL DONE,
THEY'LL BE READY FOR SOME OUTSIDE FUN!

PUPPIES, LIKE KIDS, HAVE LOTS OF EXTRA ENERGY TO PLAY.
SO THEY'LL NEED LOTS OF EXERCISE EVERYDAY.

TEACH THEM TO FETCH, TAKE THEM ON WALKS,
AND TEACH THEM TO SIT, STAY AND TALK.

MOST IMPORTANTLY OF ALL,
DON'T FORGET TO TELL THEM
"GOOD JOB!"

NOW THIS SECTION IS SUPER IMPORTANT,
SO LISTEN UP,
BECAUSE WE CAN'T STRESS THIS ENOUGH.

PUPPIES LOVE, LOVE , LOVE TO CHEW THINGS UP.

SO BE SURE TO CLEAN UP AND PUT EVERYTHING IN IT'S PLACE,

BECAUSE IF YOUR PUP IS ANYTHING LIKE BEAR,
HE'S GOING TO WANT A TASTE.

GRAB A BIG BONE OR A TASTY CHEWY TOY,
AND GIVE IT TO YOUR PUP TO DESTROY.
A GENIUS IDEA IF YOU ASK ME,
THIS NOT ONLY HELPED BEAR GROW STRONG TEETH,
BUT I FINALLY HAD HOMEWORK
THAT HE DIDN'T WANT TO EAT.

ONE LAST THING TO NOTE,
A PUP WILL ALWAYS GET DIRTY,
IT'S JUST WHAT THEY DO.
SOMETIMES IT'S FROM SILLY THINGS
LIKE FALLING ASLEEP IN THEIR FOOD.

IN SHORT, OUR PUPPIES WILL NEED LOTS OF CLEANING UP,
PAWS AND EARS SHOULD ALWAYS BE SCRUBBED.

MAKE SURE TO USE A TEARLESS SHAMPOO,
ANYTHING WITH LAVENDER WILL DO.

THE LAVENDER WILL KEEP UNWANTED FRIENDS AWAY.
BEAR REALLY APPRECIATES NOT HAVING FLEAS.
"YAY!!!"

PUPPIES ARE SO LOVING AND FUN,
BUT IT'S OUR JOB TO MAKE SURE THEY LEARN TO BE GOOD ONES.
EVERY DAY WHEN I WAKE UP,
I LIKE TO REMIND BEAR HE'S THE GREATEST PUP,
AND BEFORE WE GO TO BED, WE END EACH DAY WITH A HUG.

WELL I THINK THAT ABOUT DOES IT FOR NOW,
HOPEFULLY OUR BOOK HELPED OUT WITH YOUR NEW PAL.

NOW IS THE TIME TO BE PROUD OF YOURSELVES,
YOU'VE DONE IT, CONGRATS,

YOU'VE RAISED A GOOD PAL!!

THANK YOU FOR READING WITH US AND GOOD LUCK,

THANK YOU

and

GOODLUCK

HOW TO RAISE
AN
OUTSTANDING PUP

SIGNED BUTTONS AND BEAR,
THE OUTSTANDING PUP.

IMPORTANT DATES FOR PUPPY HEALTH

PUP NAME: ____________________ BIRTHDAY: ____________________

BREED: ____________________ VETERINARIAN: ____________________

IMMUNIZATION DATES:

Vaccine	8wks	12wks	16wks	Update
*DA2PP				Annually
Bordetella				Annually
Leptospirosis				Annually
Lyme				Annually
Rabies		AFTER 90 DAYS OLD		1yr after 1st vax every 3yrs after that

www.ingramcontent.com/pod-product-compliance
Ingram Content Group UK Ltd.
Pitfield, Milton Keynes, MK11 3LW, UK
UKHW061459070726
13610UKWH00004B/6
9798987223727